anythink

Flowchart

Smart

# The Science of
# MAGNETISM

Louise Spilsbury

**Gareth Stevens**
PUBLISHING

Please visit our website, **www.garethstevens.com**.
For a free color catalog of all our high-quality books,
call toll free 1-800-542-2595 or fax 1-877-542-2596.

Cataloging-in-Publication Data

Spilsbury, Louise.
The science of magnetism / by Louise Spilsbury.
p. cm. — (Flowchart smart)
Includes index.
ISBN 978-1-4824-4147-5 (pbk.)
ISBN 978-1-4824-4148-2 (6-pack)
ISBN 978-1-4824-4149-9 (library binding)
1. Magnetism — Juvenile literature. I. Spilsbury, Louise. II. Title.
QC753.7 S65 2016
538—d23

First Edition

Published in 2016 by
**Gareth Stevens Publishing**
111 East 14th Street, Suite 349
New York, NY 10003

© 2016 Gareth Stevens Publishing

Produced for Gareth Stevens by Calcium
Editors: Sarah Eason and Harriet McGregor
Designers: Paul Myerscough and Emma DeBanks

Cover art: Shutterstock: Denkcreative, Lineartestpilot.

Picture credits: Shutterstock: ArtisticPhoto 30–31, Art_of_sun 1, 8, Cozyta 12–13,
Daisy Daisy 40–41, Gustavo Fadel 45t, Aleksandra Gigowska 17r, Arto Hakola 24–25,
Pat Hastings 14–15, Imagesbyruthwilson 4, Imageman 34–35, Jordache 16–17,
Manfredxy 29br, Matt9122 25tr, MilanB 6–7, 20–21, 21tr, Robert Neumann 34b,
Nevodka 36–37, Pi-Lens 22–23, Snowbelle 22b, Solarseven 44–45, Takasu 8–9,
TFoxFoto 28–29, Vaclav Volrab 30b, Wlad74 5, Worradirek 13b.

Printed in the United States of America
CPSIA compliance information: Batch #CW16GS: For further information contact
Gareth Stevens, New York, New York at 1-800-542-2595.

# Contents

# Chapter 1
## What Is Magnetism?

Magnetism is an amazing and mysterious type of force. A magnet is an object or material that exerts a magnetic force. A magnet can attract, or pull, certain types of metal materials and objects toward it. It can also repel, or push, those metals away. What is special about magnetism is that it is a force that can act on other objects without even touching them. There are many different kinds of magnets but they can all exert this mysterious power!

These plastic letters are attached to small, thick, rectangular magnets so they can stick to a refrigerator door.

There are magnets in many of the things we use every day, without knowing they are there. Magnetic clasps keep purses and camera cases closed. Magnetic strips keep cabinet doors from swinging open. Magnets are also used to produce electricity, so without them our televisions, computers, phones, and other machines would not work. Motors use magnets to make them work, so there are magnets in most machines that move, such as fans, food mixers, and electric toothbrushes.

Forces that are used to push or pull objects must usually touch the material they are moving. When you want to pull a book toward you across a table, you make physical contact with it. Magnetism is a non-contact force. A magnetic material does not need to touch an object to apply its power. Magnets produce a magnetic force that can be applied through air, water, and even some solid materials, such as paper and plastic.

## Get Smart!

Historians believe that the ancient Greeks and early Chinese civilizations knew about magnetism. They each discovered a special, rare type of stone, called a lodestone, which had the power to attract iron. The word "magnetism" probably comes from an area called Magnesia in the country that is now Turkey, where ancient civilizations found many of these magnetic stones in the ground.

A lodestone is a naturally magnetic piece of a mineral called magnetite. Magnetite contains iron.

# Magnet Poles

One magnet can be used to apply two different forces: it can be used to repel magnetic objects or it can be used to attract them. How can this happen? The secret lies in a magnet's two ends, or poles.

The opposite ends of a magnet are called the poles. One end is the magnetic north pole; the other is the magnetic south pole. The magnetic force produced by a magnet is strongest near its poles. Different, or unlike, poles attract each other. If you place the south pole of one magnet near the north pole of another magnet, they will pull together. Like poles repel each other. So, if you place the south pole of one magnet near the south pole of another magnet, they push apart. People wear magnetic earrings that stay on because of magnetism. Each of the earring's two parts contains a small magnet, and when two opposite poles of the magnets face one other, they pull the two parts of the earring together through the earlobe to hold the earring on the ear.

Some magnets are stronger than others, but all magnets can only work over a certain distance. The strength of the magnetic force from the poles of a magnet becomes weaker the farther you move from the magnet. Other materials can also block the magnetism. For example, the two magnets that pull together to close a purse will only work when the opposite poles are very close together. They will no longer attract each other if something comes between them. Magnetic forces can work through many materials, but they pass more easily through some than others.

Horseshoe, or U-shaped, magnets like this have the poles side by side. The blue end of a magnet is usually the south pole. The red end of a magnet is usually the north pole.

# How Magnets Work

Magnetism is an invisible force and it is caused by tiny particles that are invisible to the human eye. Magnetism is caused by the movement of electrons. These incredibly tiny particles carry electric charges inside atoms.

Atoms are the building blocks of all matter. There are more than 100 different types of atoms in existence, and they combine in different ways to form every substance in the universe. We cannot see atoms, but scientists have discovered that an atom is made up of a central core of matter called the nucleus, which contains protons and neutrons. Electrons orbit around the nucleus in a similar way to how planets orbit around the sun in space. Electrons follow an almost circular path around the nucleus, and each electron spins around and around at the same time at incredible speeds.

This simple diagram of an atom shows the paths taken by electrons as they orbit the nucleus.

As the electrons move, they create an electric current. This makes each electron work like a very small magnet. Electrons in most atoms exist in pairs, with each electron spinning in an opposite direction. This means that the magnetic effect of one electron in a pair cancels out the effect of the other. Atoms in paper have equal pairs of electrons, which is why such materials are only very weakly magnetic. However, some metals, including iron, have atoms in which electrons are not working in pairs. When these unpaired electrons spin in the same direction in an atom, they can line up with each other and make the atom magnetic. When all the atoms in a substance create magnetic forces that pull or push in one direction, the substance becomes strongly magnetic.

This magnet contains iron, a metal in which all of the atoms create magnetic forces that pull strongly and attract the metal paper clips.

Get flowchart smart!

# Why Magnets Are Magnetic

Follow the flowchart to see why magnets are magnetic.

In *the atoms* that make up all materials, electrons orbit the nucleus.

Electrons moving in pairs in opposite directions cancel out the electric charge each creates.

Together, the atoms create a strong pulling force, which makes the material magnetic.

In a magnetic material, unpaired electrons spin in the same direction, which makes each atom behave like a mini-magnet.

S

N

The electrons in all of the atoms in the material line up, so their force is working in the same direction.

Flowchart Smart

# Chapter 2

# Magnetic Materials

Magnets attract other magnets, but they can also attract materials that are magnetic. This is how a magnet can stick to a refrigerator door. All magnetic materials are metals, but only a few metals are magnetic.

Iron is the most common magnetic material, and any metal that contains iron will be attracted to a magnet. Materials such as iron that are strongly attracted by a magnetic force are said to be ferromagnetic. Steel is also a ferromagnetic material, because it is an alloy containing iron and other metals. Most other metals, such as copper, aluminum, brass, tin, silver, and gold, are only weakly magnetic. That is why a steel food or drink can is attracted to a magnet, but aluminum cans are not attracted to a magnet. Recycling centers use magnets to sort out steel cans for recycling into steel, and aluminum cans for recycling into aluminum. You may see a magnet symbol printed on some steel cans.

In addition to iron, other ferromagnetic materials include nickel, cobalt, and some alloys of rare earth metals such as the silver-white gadolinium. These magnetic materials can become permanent magnets and retain their magnetism for a long time. For example, steel is made from a mixture of metals, and this makes steel harder than iron and causes it to keep its magnetic properties longer than iron alone.

Not all cans are magnetic. Only those that contain steel will be attracted to a magnet.

An alnico magnet is a powerful permanent-magnet alloy that contains iron, nickel, aluminum, and one or more of the elements cobalt, copper, and titanium. Alnico alloys have a high resistance to loss of magnetism, so they stay magnetic for a very long time.

This giant magnet is being used to separate, lift, and move magnetic metals quickly and easily.

# Temporary Magnets

There are two basic kinds of magnets: permanent magnets and temporary magnets. It is possible to make a new magnet by exposing a ferromagnetic metal, such as iron or nickel, to magnetic forces. When the newly magnetized metal is heated to a high temperature, it becomes a permanent magnet. It is also possible to make a temporary magnet. Temporary magnets are made from materials that are easy to magnetize, but that lose their magnetism quickly and easily. Permanent magnets are harder to make into magnets, but they are more useful because they keep their magnetism longer.

Iron nails can be made into temporary magnets. One way to do this is to hold a strongly magnetic substance against an existing magnet. For example, when you rub an iron nail along a magnet in one direction, the north-seeking poles of the atoms in the nail line up in the same direction. As the atoms line up, they create a magnetic force. The more you rub the nail along the magnet, the more north-seeking poles of the atoms line up, and the more magnetic the nail becomes. However, when you move the nail away from the magnet, it soon loses its magnetic powers.

Every object that is lifted or moved by a magnet acts as a type of temporary magnet itself. When you put a magnet near a paper clip, the magnet pulls and lines up some of the north-seeking poles of the atoms in the paper clip. This turns the paper clip into a temporary magnet because the north pole of the paper clip becomes attracted toward the south pole of the magnet. While that paper clip is held by the magnet, it acts as a magnet too, so you can add another paper clip to the first, and so on. When you move the main magnet away, all of the paper clips lose their magnetism and fall down.

The number of paper clips a magnet can hold in a line is an indication of the magnet's strength.

# Losing Magnetism

Temporary magnets lose their magnetism **easily, but** permanent magnets can lose their magnetism, too. There are ways to prevent permanent magnets from losing their magnetism.

Heat can demagnetize permanent magnets. Ferromagnetic materials, such as nickel and steel, lose all their magnetic power if they are heated to a very high temperature. Heat causes the electrons in their atoms to become too agitated to stay pointing in one direction for long. Magnetic materials lose their magnetism at different temperatures. Nickel loses its magnetism at around 660 degrees Fahrenheit (350 °C), while to remove iron's magnetism it must be heated above 1,300 degrees Fahrenheit (770 °C). Some of the strongest magnets are stored in cool places when not in use to keep **them** from losing their magnetism. A magnet can also become demagnetized if another magnet **moves** across it in different directions, **or if it is repeatedly** knocked or **dropped.**

This steel is so hot it is glowing. Nickel, steel, and other ferromagnetic materials lose their magnetism if they are heated to very high temperatures.

The magnetism of permanent magnets follows a path between the poles. If the path is made more difficult, for example if the magnetism has to travel through a gap or other nonmagnetic material, it can lose some of its strength. A horseshoe magnet has a gap between its two poles, and if it is stored as it is, it will slowly lose its power. To prevent this, an iron bar called a keeper closes the gap. The keeper forms a loop through which the magnetic forces pass, and keeps the magnet from losing its magnetic power.

If the magnetic strip on a credit card becomes demagnetized, the credit card will no longer work.

## Get Smart!

When stores swipe a credit or debit card, the black magnetic strip on the back of the card gives them all the information they need. If two cards are stored so that their magnetic strips are facing each other, the magnetic strips can become demagnetized.

Get flowchart smart!

# How Magnet Keepers Work

Follow the steps in this flowchart to understand how magnet keepers do their job.

Bar magnets are stored in boxes in pairs.

They are placed side by side with unlike poles opposite one another, so the north pole of one magnet is next to the south pole of another. This keeps them from constantly repelling each other and weakening their magnetism.

Soft iron bars called keepers are placed across the ends.

When the iron keeper touches the magnets, it becomes magnetized.

The keeper completes a loop of opposite poles for the magnetic flow to follow, and helps the bar magnets to keep their magnetism.

Flowchart Smart

# Chapter 3

# Magnetic Fields

Magnetism is a force that can act across a distance. Its power can be felt in a three-dimensional zone around the magnet. This is called the magnetic field, and every magnet is surrounded by a magnetic field. We cannot see the magnet's magnetic field, but we can see the effect that it has on other magnetic materials.

Every magnet produces a magnetic field that is stronger around its two poles. That's why the lines of iron filings being pulled toward the magnets in this picture are clustered together at the ends of the magnets. Magnetic poles are the points where the magnetic field lines begin and end.

## Get Smart!

A magnet of any size always produces a magnetic field with two poles. If you slice up a magnet, you simply get a smaller magnet with two opposite poles. You do not get one magnet with only a south pole and one magnet with only a north pole. The only thing that changes is the strength of the magnets. The two smaller magnets will not be as strong as the bigger single magnet.

Because the magnetic field of this magnet is most powerful at its poles, this is the part that attracts the thumbtacks most strongly.

A magnetic field is the area around a magnet in which it can attract or repel magnetic materials. In a magnetic field, the strength and direction of the magnetic effect varies from point to point. The field is strongest near the poles of a magnet. Although magnetic forces are invisible, they can be made visible by sprinkling iron filings around a magnet. The iron filings line up around the magnet in the shape of its magnetic field, from the north pole of a magnet to its south pole. The lines also show the strength of the magnetism over the different parts of its magnetic field. The magnetic field is stronger where the field lines are closer together. The lines are closest together at the poles, because that's where the magnetic force is strongest. Powerful magnets have a wider and larger magnetic field, which is why their magnetic force can be felt farther away. Smaller, weaker magnets only have a small magnetic field, which is why they have to be held close to metal objects to attract them.

# Earth's Magnetic Field

Did you know that Earth is a magnet? The core of our planet contains iron and nickel at temperatures so hot that some of it is in a constantly melted state. Scientists believe that rotation in the spinning liquid of the outer core creates electrical currents that produce Earth's magnetic field. Approximately every 200,000 to 5 million years, Earth's magnetic field switches positions. The north pole becomes the south pole, and the south pole becomes the north pole.

Earth is so large, and its magnetic core is buried so deep within it, that by the time its magnetic force reaches the surface its magnetism is far weaker.

Earth's magnetic field is so big that it stretches into space. It is called the magnetosphere. The force from the magnetosphere acts like a shield and protects Earth by repelling harmful rays from the sun and particles that would destroy the atmosphere if they entered it. Earth's magnetic field has field lines similar to those found around a bar magnet, just a lot, lot bigger. The magnetic north and south poles of Earth are the places where the planet's field lines come together. Unlike the points on a map that we call the North and South Pole, the magnetic north and the magnetic south poles keep moving. Although the magnetic north pole is now very close to the point on Earth we call the geographic North Pole, not long ago it was in Arctic Canada!

The aurora borealis is seen here over northern Canada at dawn as particles from the sun collide with Earth's atmosphere.

# Get Smart!

Near Earth's magnetic poles, it is often possible to see amazing displays of glowing, multicolored light patterns in the sky. Around the magnetic north pole these displays are called the aurora borealis, and around the magnetic south pole they are called the aurora australis. These incredible effects are created by Earth's magnetic field. They happen when tiny particles from the sun pass through the magnetosphere and interact with substances in the atmosphere as they follow Earth's magnetic field lines.

# Using Earth's Magnetic Field

Earth's magnetic field is very useful. Humans and animals around the world use Earth's magnetic field to navigate, or find their way around, and plan which route they want to take. Compasses containing magnets are some of the oldest navigational tools in history. They have been used by people for hundreds of years and they are still in use today.

A compass contains a small magnetic needle that sits on a pivot. The needle can spin freely in all directions. The compass needle responds to Earth's magnetism so that its needle always points to Earth's magnetic north, near the North Pole. It is important that the magnetic needle is lightweight and spins easily or it will not move easily enough to always point north. Earth's magnetic field is weak at the surface because the magnetic force has a long way to travel from the center of the planet. Thick, heavy compass needles would be unable to respond to this relatively weak force.

Arctic terns use a combination of methods to find their way during migration, such as recognizing landmarks and sensing Earth's magnetic field.

Hammerhead sharks have receptors in their uniquely shaped heads to help them sense Earth's magnetic field.

Amazingly, at least 50 types of animals use Earth's magnetic field to navigate. Animals, including some types of birds, fish, and whales, often travel long distances between feeding and breeding grounds. Arctic terns make a round trip from the North to the South Pole every year of 43,000 miles (69,200 km) and gray whales travel about 12,400 miles (19,950 km). These animals partly use landmarks, such as coastlines, the position of the sun in the day or the stars at night, and even the smell of different places to help them on their way, but they also sense variations in the angle or strength of Earth's magnetic field. Scientists are not sure exactly how it works, but it is very accurate and it's almost as though these animals have an internal compass of their own.

Get flowchart smart!

# How a Compass Works

Let's take a closer look at how compasses work using a flowchart.

A compass is placed on a flat surface.

The magnetic needle inside the compass responds to Earth's magnetic field.

The compass needle always points north, so you can rotate the compass until the "North" marking aligns with the needle. The other markings on the compass show you where east, south, and west are.

The needle moves to align itself with Earth's magnetic field.

The north end of the compass needle magnet points to the magnetic north pole, which is roughly the same as our geographic North Pole.

The south end of the compass needle magnet points to the magnetic south pole, which is roughly the same as our geographic South Pole.

Flowchart

Smart

# Chapter 4
# Electromagnetism

Electromagnets are a special and very useful type of magnet. In an electromagnet, a magnetic field is generated only when electricity flows through it.

Electricity is the flow of moving electrons. When electrons move, or hop, between different atoms within a substance, they carry electrical energy from one place to another. When electricity runs through a wire, it generates a magnetic field around that wire. If you wind the wire around a ferromagnetic metal such as iron, the magnetic field of the loops of wire increases the effect of the magnetic field. The metal becomes magnetized and turns into an electromagnet, with the strength of the magnetic field produced by the electric current coming from the coils of wire. To make an even more powerful magnetic field, you can wind the wire into tighter coils around the metal, or increase the electric current flowing through the coil. This creates a stronger electromagnet and allows you to make an electromagnet that is more powerful than normal, permanent magnets of the same size.

Electromagnets are very useful. Permanent magnets always produce the same strength of magnetic force. Electromagnets are different. They are only magnetic while an electric current is flowing through them. Once the electric current stops flowing, they are no longer magnetic. This means electromagnets can be turned on and off at the flick of a switch. Electromagnets are used in places such as junkyards and recycling centers. When the electromagnet is switched on it can attract and lift metals, and hold onto them while a crane moves them. When the electromagnet is turned off, it drops the metals in a new location.

The claw of this crane is attached to an electromagnet. It lifts and relocates iron and steel in a metal recycling yard.

The coils of copper wire around an iron core can be used to create an electromagnet.

# Generating Electricity

It is not only possible to use electricity to make magnetism. We can also use magnets to make electricity. Electricity is the flow of electrical power from atoms. Currents of electricity are created when electrons are forced to move from atom to atom. As we have seen, magnets work by generating a magnetic field that pulls and pushes electrons within the atoms of objects near them, making the electrons move. Certain metals, such as copper, have electrons that are moved easily from their orbits. By moving a magnet quickly through a coil of copper wire, the changing magnetic field makes electrons flow in the wire. Electricity is created in this generator, and the movement of power is called an electric current.

Electricity is made in giant power plants like this one, and then carried to buildings through wires.

Transmission lines carrying electricity from power plants are held safely above the ground by huge towers called transmission towers.

The electricity we use to power computers, lights, and other appliances is produced in giant power plants. Most power plants burn large amounts of coal or other fossil fuel to boil water and produce steam. The steam is funneled toward a big fan-like machine called a turbine, causing the turbine blades to spin. The spinning turbine rotates a coil of wire inside a magnetic field or spins a large, very powerful magnet inside a long coil of wire. This creates strong pulling and pushing forces in the coil of wire, which makes electrons in the wire move between atoms. An electric current flows through the wire.

## Get Smart!

Magnetism is used to control the strength of the electricity that flows to our homes. The electricity that travels out of power plants along metal cables is very powerful. Before it reaches our homes it passes through a transformer station. There, electrons pass through large coils that create magnetic fields that reduce the electricity's power, so that it is at a safe strength to use in machines.

Get flowchart smart!

# Electromagnetism Makes Electricity

Discover how magnets are used to produce electricity in power plants, following the flowchart.

Coal, gas, or oil is burned to provide heat.

Heat from the burning fuel is used to boil water in a boiler.

When free electrons are all moving in the same direction, an electric current is created.

Steam from the boiling water rises upward into turbines.

→

The steam turns the blades of the turbines.

The movement of the turbines moves a powerful magnet in a large coil of wire.

This creates a magnetic field that makes electrons break free from their atoms.

Flowchart Smart

# Chapter 5

# Magnets and Motors

When you reach for an electric toothbrush, dry your hair with a hairdryer, or cool yourself with an electric fan, you are enjoying the benefits of electromagnetism. One of the most important uses of electromagnetism is to power the electric motors that are in the machines we use every day.

An electric motor is a machine that uses electrical energy from an electrical source, such as a battery or a socket, and changes that energy into movement energy to do some type of work. Motors are used in an incredible variety of machines, from computer hard drives and DVD players, to ceiling fans and refrigerators.

When an electromagnet is used to make something spin or move, this movement can be used to make other parts of a machine spin, too. This is why motors can be used to drive moving parts in machines such as food mixers, drills, and washing machines. For example, in an electric toothbrush, an electric motor makes the metal at the top of the device, and therefore the brush head we attach to that metal, spin to clean and polish our teeth. In a vacuum cleaner, the motor turns the blades of a fan that sucks in dust and dirt from carpets.

Electromagnets create the motion in the head of your electric toothbrush, which loosens debris left behind in your teeth.

A motor with an electromagnet spins these beaters, which are being used to whip cream.

## Get Smart!

Machines need different-sized motors to do different types of work. For example, a machine that moves a large, heavy load, such as a washing machine that needs to move not only dirty laundry but also heavy loads of water, requires a more powerful motor than a machine that moves a small load, such as an electric can opener. However, all motors work on the same basic principle.

# How Motors Work

The key to grasping how an electric motor works is to understand how electromagnets can be controlled. One thing that makes electromagnets so incredibly useful is that we can change the amount of electricity that flows through them. The other smart thing about electromagnets is that we can also change the direction in which electricity flows through them. When we continually change the direction in which electricity flows through an electromagnet, we can make a motor work.

In a very simple motor, a movable loop of wire is positioned near a fixed magnet. When an electric current is passed through the wire, it becomes an electromagnet. When the south pole of the electromagnet is near the south pole of the fixed magnet, the like magnetic poles repel each other. The fixed magnet cannot move, so the electromagnet moves in the motor: its south pole moves away from the south pole of the fixed magnet. As it rotates, the south pole of the electromagnet gets nearer to the north pole of the fixed magnet and is pulled toward it because opposite magnetic poles attract each other.

Electromagnets make motors work in a huge variety of machines, including fun gadgets like this remote-controlled helicopter.

Just at the point at which the two opposite poles meet, a part called a commutator changes the direction in which the electricity is moving. When the direction of the electric current changes, the north and south poles of the electromagnet change places, too. Suddenly, the south pole of the electromagnet is near a south pole in the fixed magnet again, rather than a north pole. So the electromagnet continues to rotate as the two like poles repel each other and the two unlike poles attract each other. This happens again and again, at every half-turn of the electromagnet. This movement rotates other parts to which it is connected and causes them to move and spin and make the machine work.

Get flowchart smart!

# Electric Motors

Follow the flowchart for a closer look at how electric motors work.

An electric current flows through a coil of wire that is free to rotate between two opposite magnetic poles.

Every half-turn, the direction of the electric current is changed to keep the coil of wire moving continuously in the same direction.

The coil of wire becomes an electromagnet. When its south pole faces the south pole of the magnet around it, the magnets repel each other. This magnetic force makes the coil of wire move.

When the south pole of the coil of wire faces the north pole of the magnet, the direction of the current is reversed.

This means two south poles are facing each other again, and again the magnetic force makes the coil of wire move.

Flowchart Smart

# Chapter 6
# Magnetism and Us

Magnetism is an invisible force, but it is incredibly useful and it works for us in many different ways. It helps us power machines, navigate, travel, and even detect illness.

In just one car, there are many magnets at work. Car GPS systems require magnetism to work, and there are magnets in the motors that move the windows up and down, work the windshield wipers, adjust seats and mirrors, and start the engine. When you turn on the radio or put in a CD, magnets help you to hear music too. As pulses of electricity travel through an electromagnet in a loudspeaker, the electromagnet is attracted to and repelled by a permanent magnet. It pushes and pulls a speaker cone, making it vibrate and produce sound waves that you can hear.

A magnetic resonance imaging (MRI) scanner is a machine that can make detailed images of the soft parts inside the human body. The human body is mostly water, and water consists of hydrogen and oxygen atoms. The protons in hydrogen atoms are like tiny magnets and are very sensitive to magnetic fields. When a patient lies in the MRI scanner, they are surrounded by a large, tube-shaped electromagnet, which causes the protons in the body to line up in the same direction, in the same way that a magnet pulls the needle of a compass. Then the machine sends radio waves to the part of the body to be tested, and this disturbs the protons. When this happens, a computer figures out where the protons are and what tissue they are part of. It uses this information to create images of the inside of the body to see whether any damage or disease is present.

A magnetic resonance imaging scan of the head uses powerful magnets and radio waves to create pictures of the brain like this one. MRI scans can highlight problems with blood flow, blood vessels, and brain activity.

Get flowchart smart!

# How MRI Scanners Work

Follow the flowchart for a closer look at MRI scanners.

A patient lies down inside an MRI scanner.

The scanner is switched on and an electromagnet creates a magnetic field.

Doctors use this information to figure out whether there are any problems in body parts such as the brain, lungs, or heart.

The magnetic field causes the protons in hydrogen atoms in the water that makes up the human body to line up in the same direction.

Radio waves disturb the protons and when they line up again they bounce back radio signals, which a computer picks up.

The computer can then figure out where each atom is, and even what type of tissue it belongs to.

Flowchart Smart

# Magnetism in the Future

Humans have been using magnetism ever since its discovery, and we are finding new ways to use its powers all the time. In the future, we could all be driving electric cars, and astronauts could be launched into space from a magnetic launchpad. Magnets may even be able to help us solve one of the major problems facing the world today: water shortage.

Electric cars do not look different than ordinary cars, but they are powered by an electric motor instead of a gasoline engine. Electric cars produce fewer of the gases that become trapped in our atmosphere and contribute to climate change. More countries may also start to use maglev trains. These trains use magnetism to float, without friction, on top of a special track, resulting in a faster and more efficient method of transport. It is also possible that the magnetic technology used to make maglev trains may also be used to create magnetic tracks and ramps to launch rockets into space. This would save some of the vast amounts of fuel required to launch a spacecraft into space today.

Some scientists think magnets could be used to upset the electrical sensors that sharks use to navigate. It may eventually be possible to use this technology to move sharks away from a populated area.

## Get Smart!

In some places where there is a shortage of freshwater, magnets are being used to remove the salt from salt water so that it can be used to irrigate crops. Electromagnets are attached to a stainless steel pipe that is connected to a water source. When water passes through the magnetic field inside the pipe, atoms within the salt particles in the water vibrate and break down. The salt is no longer hard and harmful to crops, so the water is safe to use.

Electromagnets are used in electric cars such as this hybrid supercar. Increased use of electric cars could reduce the pollution entering Earth's atmosphere from gasoline-powered cars.

# Glossary

**alloy** a metal made from a mixture of metals

**atoms** the smallest particles of a substance that can exist by itself

**commutator** a device in an electrical machine that can reverse the direction of the electric current

**compasses** devices with magnetic needles that always point north

**core** the center

**demagnetize** to take away a magnet's magnetism

**electric current** a steady flow of electrons

**electromagnets** magnets that work when electric currents pass through them

**electrons** tiny parts of an atom that have negative electric charges

**energy** the ability or power to do work

**ferromagnetic** a material that is attracted to magnets or can be made into a permanent magnet

**fossil fuel** a fuel such as oil, coal, or gas that takes millions of years to form beneath the ground

**generator** a machine that creates electricity

**keeper** a device used to keep a magnet from losing its magnetism

**magnet** a material, usually metal, that can causes invisible pulling or pushing forces

**magnetic field** an area around a magnet where its magnetism is felt

**motors** devices that produce movement to make machines work

**navigate** to find your way

**neutrons** the small parts of an atom that have no electric charge

**nucleus** the center of an atom

**orbit** to follow a circular path around an object

**permanent magnets** magnets that attract magnetic materials with the same strength until they are damaged

**pivot** a pin or point around which something else moves

**poles** the two points, north and south, at opposite ends of a magnet or at the opposite ends of Earth

**protons** the small parts of an atom that have a positive electric charge

**radio waves** invisible waves that can travel through air and carry signals

**resistance** a measure of how well an object restricts the flow of current or magnetism

**temporary magnets** magnets made from materials that are easy to magnetize but lose their magnetism quickly and easily

**transformer** a device that increases or decreases voltage

**turbine** a machine that is turned by wind, water, or steam

# For More Information

## Books

Loria, Laura. *What Is Magnetism?* (Let's Find Out! Physical Science). New York, NY: Rosen Educational Services, 2014.

Madgwick, Wendy. *Magnets & Sparks* (First Science Library). San Francisco, CA: Armadillo Books, 2014.

Meachen Rau, Dana. *Electricity and Magnetism* (21st Century Skills Library: Real World Science). North Mankato, MN: Cherry Lake Publishing, 2014.

Taylor-Butler, Christine. *Magnets* (Explorer Library: Science Explorer). North Mankato, MN: Cherry Lake Publishing, 2013.

## Websites

Read more about Earth's magnetism at:
**education.nationalgeographic.com/education/encyclopedia/magnetism/?ar_a=1**

Visit the Magnet Academy to learn more about magnetism:
**nationalmaglab.org/education/magnet-academy**

Discover more about electric motors at:
**www.explainthatstuff.com/electricmotors.html**

# Index